NEW GRAD
JOB HACKS

THE COMPLETE GUIDE TO GETTING
A JOB AFTER YOU FINISH COLLEGE

MATT TRAN FROM

"A man who views the world the same at fifty as he did at twenty has wasted thirty years of his life."

- Muhammad Ali

This book is dedicated to the people that subscribed to my YouTube channel when I first started out. You believed in me when I doubted myself.

CONTENTS

INTRODUCTION

In the summer of 2009, I celebrated my 21st birthday the same way any college student hopes to: with a stupid amount of binge drinking. It was an epic four night marathon of drinking with friends. One month later, I finished my last classes for my Bachelor's of Psychology and Social Behavior. I had accomplished what every young adult hopes to accomplish: getting a college education. Then I realized what every young adult realizes after graduation: I've learned nothing.

My grades for my last classes were Bs. I hadn't read a single book that quarter. I just skimmed the books before the exams and chose the multiple choice answer that made the most sense. I hadn't completed a reading assignment since my sophomore year. Usually, after the first midterm I could predict what the professor was going to put on the exam. Good enough to get a GPA above 3.0.

I constantly got reminders to reserve my cap and gown for graduation. Celebrations are for real achievements, so I didn't walk. A couple months later, my classmates messaged me asking what classes I was taking for the Fall semester. Nobody knew I graduated except for my parents.

I was lost. The resources online were inadequate (they still are), and every college adviser I visited made me feel more lost. My parents gave me the typical career advice: Healthcare or Engineering. None of the advice I got made sense, and most of it was outdated, which is why I'm writing this book– to be the first handbook that gives realistic career advice that is supported with data and proof.

Now it's the winter of 2015. I currently work as the main content creator for Chameleon.LA, one of the best growth hacking & social media management companies in Los Angeles. I create memes (a piece of media that is shareable) for big YouTubers and companies. One of my clients is Bro Science Life, a YouTube channel that currently has 1.5 million subscribers. I made viral internet memes for Uproxx.com, which regularly got 10 million+ views. Before I stepped into the media world, I got a degree in mechanical engineering and worked as an engineer in three different industries: natural gas, oil, and HVAC.

While getting fired from all three jobs, I created the most popular career channel on YouTube: Engineered Truth. I currently have 60,000 subscribers that rely on me for career information that they can't get anywhere else. Now I'm going to share with you how to get your first real job– and no, you don't have to become an engineer, doctor or lawyer.

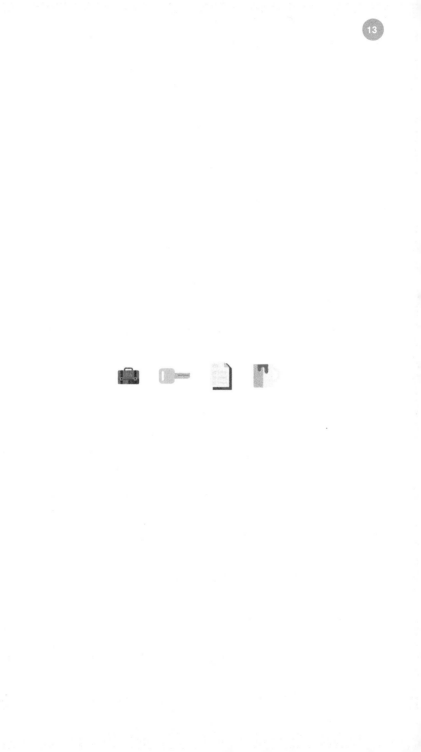

CHAPTER 1 //
I Got A Useless Degree...Now What?

I Got A Useless Degree…Now What?//
How to Turn Your Miscellaneous
Degree into a Career

"We ask 18-year-olds to make huge decisions about their career and financial future, when a month ago they had to ask to go the bathroom."
-Adam Kotsko

When I started college, I was extremely optimistic about my future. There was no doubt in my mind that college would be the best investment of my life. Three years later, it turned into one of my biggest regrets. During the third year of my psychology and social behavior program, I realized that I had learned almost no practical skills and probably wouldn't learn any by the time I graduated. You could say I went senile earlier than most students about their career. When I was about to graduate, I felt cheated and lied to. To me, college was a huge propaganda scam because most degrees don't teach any practical skills.

Most graduating college students are overly optimistic about how prepared they are for the working world. In a survey by Hart's Research Associates, only 26% of college students said that their college needed to improve on preparing students for entry-level jobs. Unfortunately, employers don't agree. 58% of employers said that colleges needed to do more to prepare students for entry-level jobs.

College is a confusing place. Most students graduate extremely optimistic about their future. 74% of college students say that college is adequately preparing them for real life. Yet 80% of workers in their 20s say they want to change careers, and 73% say they never landed the job they wanted (http://www.huffingtonpost.com/2013/07/01/workers-change-careers_n_3530346.html). Nearly 8% are jobless, and a staggering 44% are underemployed (have jobs that don't require a degree).

It's Not All About The Degree

There are a lot of transitions in life to be excited for. Going off to college, moving out of your parents' house, getting married, having kids. Then there's getting your first real job. Getting your first real job is a lot like getting six pack abs. People that have them make it look easy, you think you can do it in just 90 days, and it takes 10x more effort than you thought it would. It's the one rough transition in life that some people never recover from. It's fairly common for me to meet people who are in their 30s who still don't have a job that they find fulfilling. My primary goal with this book is to not have that happen to you.

Unless you're graduating with one of the few useful college degrees (engineering, nursing, accounting, etc.), you probably feel the same way I did when I graduated with a psychology and social behavior degree. I studied my butt off, wrote a lot of essays that I never cared for, and still graduated with no practical skills. I thought about going to grad school until I found out that the only schools that had a clinical psychology program were private schools with a $200,000 price tag. The declining demand for psychologists didn't help either. The numbers were not in my favor.

But things aren't that bad. There's one thing I wish someone told me after I graduated: **Colleges can't keep up with how fast the job market is changing. So now companies are looking for specific skills instead of specific degrees. There are a number of jobs that only came about within the past five years and because they're so new, there are no college degrees that teach the required skills.** Here are two new careers that require no degree.

UX/UI
DESIGNER

 SKILLS

 User Experience Design

Photoshop

Visual Design

Wireframes and prototyping

 COMPENSATION

 $70K – $110K Salary

 REQUIRED SKILLS/EXPERIENCE

 A portfolio of awesome UX/UI design and can share your strategy and process.

 Excellent visual design skills with sensitivity to human-centered experiences.

- 📌 Great understanding of branding / able to create a consistent brand identity for our products.

- 📌 Accustomed to validating designs through both user and A/B testing—mixing both qualitative and quantitative design feedback into your process.

- 📌 Flexible when it comes to trying new approaches.

- 📌 Ability to effectively manage time, prioritize tasks and work within deadlines with little supervision.

- 📌 Strong communication skills needed to provide direction and to establish best practices within the team.

- 📌 Thrive in highly collaborative, fluid, fast-paced open office environment.

- 📌 Fluent in Adobe creative products.

- 📌 Basic knowledge of HTML and CSS.

UX/UI Designers are professionals who design how an app or software looks. They make mockups and wireframes (sketch drawings) to help software engineers design an app. They also get feedback from users to see how people are using their app (very psychology-based). The post above shows a salary range of $70k- $110k; this is a common range for experienced UX/UI professionals. Best of all, no degree needed. The best way to get your foot in the door as a UX/UI designer is to take a bootcamp at a coding school.

UX/UI
JOB TRENDS

UX/UI

Indeed.com searches millions of jobs from thousands of job sites.
This job trends graph shows the percentage of jobs we find that
contain your search terms.

AdWords is an online service that Google provides where companies can pay to be on the top of search results. In 2012, Google's total advertising revenues were $43.7 billion, which averages to $120 million a day. Companies are spending a lot of money to show up on search results, and they want to make sure that they're getting a return on investment. To do so, they'll hire ad operation managers and specialists to create the ads, track their success, and to find new ways to advertise online.

AD OPERATIONS &
OPTIMIZATION MANAGER

SKILLS

- Ad operations
- Mobile apps

COMPENSATION

- $65K – $75K Salary

MARKETS

- Social Games
- Music
- Films
- Mobile Games

JOB DESCRIPTION

OPTIMIZATION

Maximize revenue from ad inventory across mobile and social apps.

- Hands-on metrics pulling from dashboards and analysis to determine best weighting and networks for each platform, ad type and country.

- Perform quantitative and qualitative analysis of key performance metrics and report findings to product management and executive teams.

- Expanding Ad Revenue Opportunities.

- Manage relationships with vendors and ad networks, keeping abreast of deal inflows, accountability and delivery to contract terms and expectations.

AD OPERATIONS

- Create and test new ad placements and networks implementing custom campaigns and sponsorships.

- Set up and oversee quality concern process.

 ## REQUIRED SKILLS/EXPERIENCE

- One or more years in mobile advertising from the publisher side of the business.

- Experience with ad trafficking, ad networks and ad intermediation services (experience with MoPub a plus).

- Adept at understanding platform analytics to strategize on campaign optimization and placement.

- Strong analytical and Excel/Google spreadsheet skills.

- Familiar with online ad serving concepts (CPM/CPA/RTB/ROI), mobile, social, video a plus.

Ad Operations positions will almost never ask for a specific degree because there's no college that teaches it. I wouldn't even recommend a business marketing degree because most of the classes wouldn't be relevant to ad operations. You'll learn much more by doing this job at a small company than you ever will at a university. Glassdoor states that the national average salary is $62,592.

AD OPERATIONS SALARIES & JOB TRENDS

SALARY
National Average
62,592K

MIN 43K — MAX 89K

AD OPERATIONS

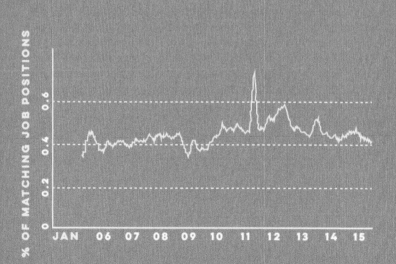

% OF MATCHING JOB POSITIONS

JAN 06 07 08 09 10 11 12 13 14 15

I get a lot of emails from people who feel like they can't do anything with their degree. I usually point them in the direction of a new age career like the two I mentioned above for two reasons: 1. They don't have to go back to school, and 2. These careers are still fairly unknown and unsaturated. Usually, they're really skeptical because they've never heard of these careers, and so they're set on getting a second bachelor's in accounting, engineering or healthcare. I respond by showing them graphs that will change their mind.

Getting a Technical Degree is So 2009

Mechanical engineering, electrical engineering, and pharmacy have been trending downward since 2009. Accounting jobs have been trending downward since 2006. Engineering and accounting jobs are slowly declining because: 1. People saw that these careers made a lot of money, so a lot of people went into those fields and saturated the job market, and 2. Many mechanical engineering, electrical engineering and accounting problems are now solved or being solved by software programs. As for pharmacy, there's only so much demand for pharmacists. Pharmacy school enrollment is still skyrocketing because many people are unaware of how saturated the pharmacy field is. I'm also fairly certain that pharmacists will eventually be replaced by pharmacy robots. **Choosing a career is like choosing a stock. Once everyone knows it's a good idea, it's probably not a good idea.**

JOB TRENDS

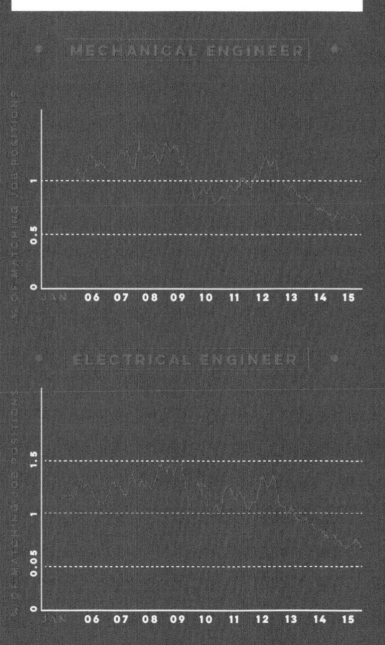

MECHANICAL ENGINEER

% OF MATCHING JOB POSITIONS

1

0.5

0

JAN 06 07 08 09 10 11 12 13 14 15

ELECTRICAL ENGINEER

% OF MATCHING JOB POSITIONS

1.5

1

0.05

0

JAN 06 07 08 09 10 11 12 13 14 15

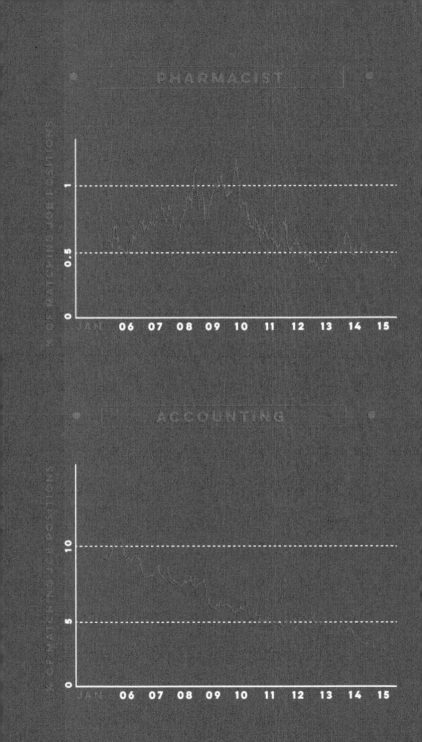

College Ain't All That Bad

Even though I've mostly been bashing college up until now, there are still a few good reasons to go to college that are hard to pass up:

College is several years of social skills condensed into four years.

There are a lot of college students who believe that socializing is a waste of time, and their only goal is to get good grades and graduate quickly. I shake my head when students do this. They're missing one of the most important things college can teach: some damn good social skills. College is a place that makes socializing easy. You can say inappropriate stuff without severe consequences– unlike a workplace where a compliment ("hey those pants make your legs look good") can easily be taken as harassment. When I was young, I underestimated the importance of social skills. There are a number of jobs (even engineering jobs) that I got because of my social skills.

College is a bridge to real life.

A high school student going straight into the working world is like pushing someone into an ice-cold pool. Working 40 hours a week at an entry-level job is not glamorous and is usually a rude awakening to the fact that they know nothing. College is a way for people to prepare for real life in a much more gentle way. Internships are a great way for people to try out a field without having to commit. Internships also tend to be easier to get because the agreement is short term and companies can let go of interns a lot easier than full-time employees. Most companies see internships as a way to test for potential full-time positions - which is a much better process than trying to assess if someone is a good fit from just interviews. College is a bridge to real life. Some people enjoy the experience and have a fun time crossing the bridge. Some people can't handle it and jump off. And some people never want to cross.

CHAPTER 2 //
Finding the Right Career

Finding the Right Career //
Basics for Finding Your Dream Job

Finding the right career is a lot like dating. You've got to try out a lot of options before you figure out what you like and don't like. There's no such thing as a perfect job, and there will always be parts of a job that you don't like. But finding your ideal job is as close as it gets to being perfect. An ideal job makes you feel complete, and you couldn't imagine it getting much better anywhere else. There are going to be ups and downs, just like a relationship, but there's no doubt in your mind that it's worth it because it aligns with your long-term goals. Your ideal job should make you feel comfortable, welcome, and should help you grow as a person–just like a relationship.

Trial and Error

Since I have one of the larger career channels on YouTube, you can imagine that I get a few emails about choosing a career. Here's the most common trend that I've noticed: **People who have never had a job before are the most lost. People who have tried a lot of different jobs have a lot better idea of what they want to do. Even if those jobs were completely irrelevant to what they decided to do for the rest of their life.**

The main reason I'm so driven to help people find their ideal career is because I had a long road to find a job I like. I feel like if I'd had some guidance, it could have made that journey a lot easier. Here's a list of jobs I've had:

 Round Table Pizza Associate (I did all the roles except delivery.)

 Orientation Leader (I gave incoming college students a tour around the campus and also did workshops to prepare them for college.)

 Home Tutor

Region Associate Engineer Intern (Fancy paperwork pusher.)

 Network Operations Center Analyst Intern (I was just a fancy graveyard shift security guard that also helped with late night tech support calls.)

 Reservoir Engineer Intern (I mostly programmed oil data into excel to make fancy graphs. They were super nice graphs. I was very proud of them.)

 HVAC Design Engineer (I drew out ducting for houses and apartment buildings in CAD software.)

 YouTube Videographer (I created tutorial and product videos for a ecommerce store.)

 Social Media Manager (I made internet memes.)

YouTube Content Creator (I make videos that give realistic career information.)

Every job I had guided me to having the two dream jobs that I have right now (Social Media Manager and YouTube Content Creator). I learned from my Round Table Pizza job that I enjoy interacting with customers. When I was an orientation leader, I found out that I enjoyed speaking in front of people– so that got me thinking I could talk in front of a camera for YouTube. I also really liked that the information I was giving to college students would help their future, which is what eventually got me to make Engineered Truth. I didn't enjoy being a home tutor, so that's when being any sort of teacher went out the window. Even now when I think about trying to teach kids… I cringe. I didn't enjoy ANY of the technical/engineering positions I had. You might be wondering why I tried so many of them if I didn't enjoy the first one. A large part of me thought it was necessary to have a technical skill like engineering to earn a high income. I later learned that there was a lot of potential money in social media and YouTube because it's a rapidly growing industry.

After I got fired from my last engineering job, I decided that I wasn't going to be dumb and try another engineering job. At the time, I had already been working on my channel for two years, so I wanted to take it to the next level. I was only making about $400 a month from my channel. I was living with my parents and that was still barely enough to get by. After a few months of taking it full-time, I was disappointed with its growth. I was only making about $600 a month, and gaining about 3,000 subscribers a month when I was hoping to get around 10,000 subscribers a month. But something good came out of me taking YouTube full-time: I got good at making videos.

I had barely been using a DSLR for a few months. I wasn't super confident in my abilities, but I figured there had to be a small company that needed someone to make their YouTube videos for them. I was willing to work for cheap. It didn't take long for me to find a job at BikeBerry.com. There, I made tutorial and product promotion videos for the company's YouTube channel. There's a lot that I learned there:

- Getting paid $15/hr to learn is a great deal. I learned a lot faster working for a company than I did on my own. I had to make different types of videos than the ones I was used to. I had to write a script, a practice I later used on my own channel.

- There's bosses out there that are bearable and perhaps even pleasant to work under. My boss at BikeBerry was the best boss I've had so far. He let us wear whatever we wanted to work. He always controlled his anger even when things went terribly wrong. He created a work environment where we felt like we were all friends just hanging out.

Film degrees are worthless. Nine months later, I quit. I still enjoyed the work, but making $15/hr wasn't fun anymore. During my time there, my skills greatly increased while my pay didn't. (If this happens to you, it's time to jump ship.) When I was looking for my replacement, I interviewed a number of people with film degrees. I was surprised at how bad these film graduates were at making basic videos. I was better than most of these applicants– even when my YouTube channel was just a hobby. If you ever considered getting a film degree, I highly recommend not to. YouTube tutorials and practicing on your own are much better teachers than a film school.

Uproxx.com (a media publisher) was looking for someone to manage their YouTube channel. I felt that with my nine months at BikeBerry and three years of working on Engineered Truth, I would be the perfect candidate for that role. I was ecstatic that I was able to interview for the position. Unfortunately, they found someone else for that role. I was bummed. Three weeks later, they called me and wanted to create a position for me: social media manager. The company's rivals had huge Instagram accounts with 200,000+ followers. Uproxx had a staggering 954 followers. They had a problem, and they thought I had the potential to solve it. I gained 11,000 organic followers in two months. It's safe to say I made a good impression. The moral of the story is that I had to try eight jobs before I found a job that I actually liked.

Class is a Terrible (Terrible) Place to Pick a Career

My favorite subject in high school was AP Physics. I know that's hard to believe. Nobody else in my class liked that class either except one other classmate named Ben. Ben and I were the only ones to pass the AP exam that year. Naturally, I chose mechanical engineering as a career since it was the application of physics. That makes sense right? I like a subject in school so I should pick that as a career. WRONG. WRONG. I COULDN'T HAVE BEEN MORE WRONG.

Working as a mechanical engineer was nothing like doing mechanical physics in class. Physics questions were fun; I was a detective trying to solve physical problems using equations and formulas. When I worked as an engineer, I was doing routine paperwork that barely felt like engineering. I was expecting engineering to be a mental challenge where I was constantly solving hard problems. Instead, I was just doing technical paperwork. I was hoping that a software engineer who was working on software would replace me.

Finding the Right Job

If you're unsure what you want to do as a career, here's what worked for me - or what I wish I had done:

- When you've never had a job, it's not time to be choosy. Take anything you can get.

- Try as many entry-level jobs that sound reasonably enjoyable. One regret that I have is that I never tried being a bartender. I would've learned a lot from it.

- Quit a job if your job makes your life miserable. I remember when I worked as an engineer intern for SoCal Gas. Every day I would struggle to get out of bed. I woke up angry and depressed. At one point, I was putting 25% of my income away into a 401k because I could retire a few years earlier. If you're counting the years toward your retirement when you're in 20s, it's time to leave. Even if you've only been at that job for a month, leave if you can. If you don't put it on your resume, nobody will even notice.

  Side note: I still have days when I want to sleep in and don't want to get out of bed even though I do like my job. After a while, I got accustomed to having a good job.

Don't worry about starting pay. When I was looking for a job, I was obsessed with getting a high salary because I thought it was necessary to be happy in life. A lot of low-income jobs have the potential to lead to higher income jobs. Bartending can lead to owning bars. Being a nail technician can lead to owning nail salons. (If you're a male, you'd be surprised at how much nail salons make.) My YouTube income started at only a couple cents a day. Now I make $50 a day. My channel also landed me the deal with Mango Media to write this book. Everything you start on your own starts small.

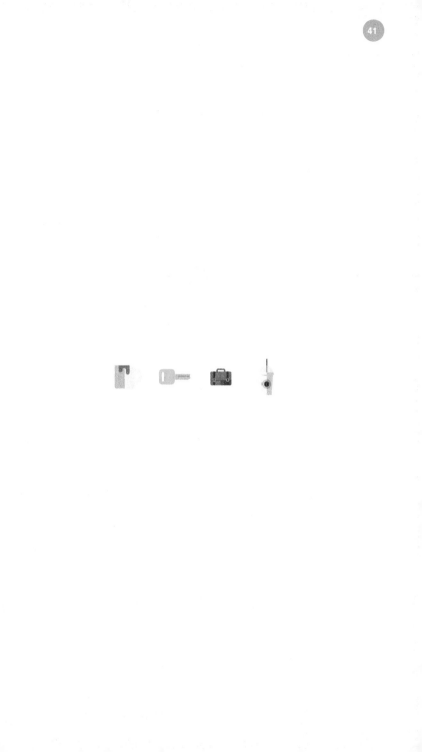

CHAPTER 3 //
Preparing Materials

Preparing Materials //
A Crash Course on Cover Letters,
Resumes and More

RESUME

There are two main ways to create a resume these days. The first is the traditional resume template that looks something like this:

Matt Tran, EIT

1425 Clark Ave., Apt# 311, Long Beach, CA 90815 · (909)210-7296 · engineeredtruth@gmail.com

Education

Pursuing Bachelor of Science in Mechanical Engineering, California State University, Long Beach

August 2010 - Present

Cumulative GPA: **3.49**
Graduating May 17, 2013 (Spring 2013)

Earned A letter grade in:
· Thermodynamics   ·Heat Analysis   · Senior Design
· Engineering CAD   ·Fluid Dynamics   · Mechanical Dynamics
· Power Plant Design   ·Finite Element Methods

Bachelor of Arts in Psychology & Social Behavior, University of California, Irvine

Sept. 2008 - Aug. 2009

Graduated summer 2010
Research Assistant for cortisol and memory study

Work Experience

Southern California Gas Company, Sempra Energy
Region Associate Engineer Intern

June 2011 - June 2012

Analyzed gas flow using software
Hands-on experience with almost all fluid control devices
Updated pipelines models from as-built sketches
Trained in ethics & compliance

Orientation Services, Cal Poly Pomona, CA
Orientation Leader

Jan.2007 - Aug. 2007

Managed large groups of people
Facilitated academic and social workshops
Encouraged students to make connections & network
Promoted student-life on campus

Technical

Engineer in Training, NCEES
Passed the fundamentals of Engineering Exam (FE) in
Mechanical Engineering

Proficient in the following software:
· Solidworks   ·Abaqus   ·Matlab   · AutoCAD   · MSOffice: Word, PowerPoint, Excel, Outlook

Activities

Human Powered Vehicle Challenge, *American Society of Mechanical Engineers*

current

Designed and fabricated a Human Powered Vehicle
Places 13th out of 29 universities
2nd place in Mac Short competition

Alpha Kappa Psi, *Professional Business Fraternity*

current

Director of Professional Programs
Rush Chair
Alpha class Vice-President

Matt Tran, EIT
306 Via Amarilla, San Dimas, CA 91773
(909) 210-7296
engineeredtruth@gmail.com

Work Experience

▌UPROXX - Social Media Contributor (June 2015 - Present)
  ▌Increased Instagram followers from 930 to 11,000 in 9 weeks with little cross-platform promotion (Instagram.com/UPROXX)
  ▌Increased Vine loops from 0 to 175,000 in 5 weeks (Vine.co/UPROXX)
  ▌Both platforms I worked on by myself

▌BikeBerry - YouTube Video Creator (Oct 2014 - July 2015)
  ▌https://www.youtube.com/watch?v=erfyYgo0bMI
  ▌https://www.youtube.com/watch?v=oQBFBdhFSJE
  ▌https://www.youtube.com/watch?v=P8WQxMwYWY

▌Engineered Truth - Owner & Video Creator
  ▌YouTube channel with 60,000 subscribers
  ▌350,000 Monthly views
  ▌1.7 Million Minutes Watched per Month
  ▌https://www.youtube.com/watch?v=SxHowT0knT4
  ▌https://www.youtube.com/watch?v=KP2YMxabxsE

Editing Experience

▌Adobe Premiere Pro: Advance
  ▌Color Correction
  ▌Color Grading

▌Adobe After Effects: Intermediate
  ▌Kinetic Typography
  ▌Masking & Moving Images
  ▌Camera Control, Lens Blur, & Lighting

Education

▌Bachelors in Mechanical Engineering, Cal State, Long Beach
  ▌3.5 GPA Cum Laude

I'm a big proponent of this new style of resume. Part of the reason is because I invented it. Most of the reason is because it's efficient and straight to the point. It keeps the resume simple and clean and if the recruiter wants to learn more, they can click on a link to see an example. One problem I saw with the traditional resume is that it didn't give the employer an idea of what a candidate was actually capable of. Someone can work at a company for three years and still not make any major contributions. It's hard to tell who would produce better work when all you can see are self-reported credentials.

Steps to building a strong resume:

Make your resume in Google Docs. When you apply to jobs, send your resume as a link to your Google Docs. The reason I like to do this is so I can update my resume after it has been sent to the recruiter. There have been times when a recruiter didn't contact me until six months after I submitted my resume! I like the flexibility of being able to change my resume at any time so that it is up to date whenever the recruiter opens it. For a lot of career portals, you have to attach a resume. I would definitely attach a resume. Always use .pdf format because it doesn't change no matter what program opens it - whereas .docx and other formats generally do. If there's a spot to write a comment, I would write: "For the most up to date resume, check out: https://docs.google.com/document/d/12HQj-FZRIQbZ4zpJlGS457UOXWkQgnvVSbuBoYXCRA4/edit?usp=sharing (That's a link to my resume; as long as I don't delete that file, it should be up to date no matter when you read this book).

Every time you complete a major project, take a bunch of pictures of it and remember to keep any documentation. We'll come back to this for the hyperlinks. If you haven't accomplished any major projects in your field, it's time to start doing one. No one wants to hire someone without any experience. There are some fields that aren't friendly to this, such as healthcare. However, there's always something you can do. The best thing you can do for a healthcare resume is go on a trip to a developing country to provide volunteer medical services. It shows true passion and commitment to serving others. When you're there, be sure to take pictures. Recruiters love pictures.

 Make your resume a similar style to the one I included above. If you're in school, your education should be on top. If you've graduated, then work experience should be on top.

Put all your documentation (pictures, reports, videos) online and put links to it on your resume. Ideally, you want a link for every bullet point you make. This will actually reduce the words necessary on your resume because now you don't have to describe what you did. Instead, you show them.

Use minimal words on your resume. Recruiters have to go through hundreds of resumes. Help them out by making their lives easy.

Include numbers. Employers want to see the impact you made. Saying you "increased sales" doesn't tell the recruiter much because you haven't measured your results. But if you say: "Increased sales by 20% in six months by using social media," now the employer will respect your abilities.

Eventually, you want everything on your resume to be 100% relevant to your industry. If you're barely getting your first internship or full-time job, leave your part-time jobs (e.g. bartending, McDonalds, Starbucks) on there because it shows responsibility and accountability. After your first job in your career, you should start chipping away at anything irrelevant.

Cover Letter

Just like the resume, there are two ways to write a cover letter: the traditional way and the modern way. The traditional way looks like this:

It uses fluffy language and has a sense of formality.

December 23, 2012

Dear [NAME OF EMPLOYER]

Today on the Cal State Long Beach Career Website, I found your available position at [NAME OF COMPANY] Aerospace Systems. Enclosed is my resume for the position for Jr. Mechanical Engineer. In review of the attached resume, you will find that I am highly capable of this role, and would be a great fit for your company, a growing leader in manufacturing.

I am currently a senior Mechanical Engineer student with a GPA of 3.46. I will be graduating in late May 2013, and will be available to work full-time as soon as I graduate. In the meantime, I am available to work 20 or more hours per week. In Engineering Graphics class, I designed complex components using CAD software. In my Manufacturing Processes class, I designed mechanical components on Solidworks then crafted them in the CSULB Lab using mills, lathes, drill press, shear press, buffer, and other manufacturing tools. In my CAD/CAM class, I worked in a team to design a rocket transporter, further improving my Solidworks abilities, and also learned NX. In addition, I also learned all the necessary basics about CAM, which will allow me to be ready for any challenges given to me. Though I have never been formally taught Inventor or Solidedge, my expertise in Solidworks and NX will transfer well into learning new CAD/CAM software.

While working at Southern California Gas as an Engineer Intern, I learned in depth about manufactured products from the consumer side. That experience will give me a clear understanding of the customer's needs. I also worked heavily in Excel for pipeline data, and feel completely comfortable with any excel project given to me. I created a number of advance spreadsheets using script/code to reduce time other engineers had to spend in excel. I am a confident writer, and would quickly adapt to technical writing.

I have a strong interest in performance parts and working at [NAME OF COMPANY] Aerospace Systems would give me the opportunity to gain experience in my dream field. I am eager to contribute to your company, and I am positive a personal interview would more accurately show my qualifications. Attached is a copy of my resume, please do not hesitate to contact me through cell phone or e-mail for any reason. Thank you for your time and consideration.

Dear Company X

I would make a good video education specialist because I already educate 60,000 subscribers every week. I run the most popular career information channel on YouTube (www.youtube.com/EngineeredTruth). I teach millennials everything we should know that's not taught in schools.

I'm currently a social media manager for Uproxx.com, a male-focused media publisher. I manager their Instagram (www.instagram.com/Uproxx) & Vine account (Vine.co/Uproxx). Prior to working at Uproxx, I created tutorial videos for 2 e-commerce stores (www.youtube.com/-BikeBerrycom & www.youtube.com/growace). Any of the videos made in the past year were made by me.

I know this cover letter is short, but I believe my links show a good example of what I can do. I could make a great video education specialist because of my years of making educational videos. If I seem like a good fit, give me a call at (909)210-7296 at any time and I'd be happy to come in for an interview.

Regards,
Matthew Tran

A modern cover letter is more conversational and is similar to an email that you would write to your professor. The traditional cover letter worked for me around 2007, but gradually got me fewer and fewer interviews. I realized that the world was shifting more towards the modern cover letter. After I updated my cover letter to a modern style, I started getting a lot more calls back. Let's go over how to make a cover letter:

The cover letter is broken down into three paragraphs:

Introduction

Always start with a hook. Your first sentence should hook the recruiter so that they want to read more about you. Always keep in mind that recruiters receive hundreds of these for every position, and if you don't hook them in the first sentence, they likely won't read the rest. In the example I included above," I would make a good video education specialist because I already educate 60,000 subscribers every week," is a good example because:

1. It tells the recruiter what I'm applying for. This is especially good if you e-mail them directly, since they might not know what position you are applying for.

2. It tells the recruiter that 47,000 other people already watch my videos, which gives me social proof.

3. It generates a bit of curiosity so that the recruiter will want to read more about me.

Qualifications

Make sure the qualifications you write align perfectly with the job the requirements. It's helpful to use their exact wording. If they say they need someone that knows how to do AutoCAD modeling, then specifically say you learned AutoCAD modeling in class or at an internship. By using their wording, you show that you didn't just copy and paste a generic cover letter. Some employers do a keyword search, so it's important to use their wording so that you show up on their search results. I recommend writing individual cover letters for every job that you apply to when you first begin your job search. After you've written 30+, then you can start mashing them together to save time.

Conclusion and Ask for an Interview

The last paragraph is fairly straight forward. Wrap up everything you said, and ask for an interview. Make it as easy as possible for them to contact you and schedule an interview.

Feel free to use the two samples I included as templates until you find your own way of writing a cover letter that aligns with your personality.

LinkedIn

LinkedIn is a website where people can make professional profiles to connect with either companies or other professionals. It's like Facebook with a career twist to it. I recommend building a LinkedIn ASAP. It's fairly dreadful to start one. LinkedIn will ask more questions about you than eHarmony (not that I would know). Most companies will want to see a LinkedIn profile - especially for jobs on the higher end. A LinkedIn profile is beneficial in these ways:

It allows employers to find you. Once you get decently well-known or experienced in your field, there's a decent chance that recruiters will reach out to you for an interview.

LINKEDIN PROFILE

Matthew Tran

Social Media at UPROXX

Greater Los Angeles Area | Marketing and Advertising

Current	YouTube, UPROXX
Previous	Niche Webstores, Inc., Cal Poly Pomona
Education	California State University–Long Beach

Send a message ▾

234
connections

1st

Background

 Summary

I currently run the Instagram account for UPROXX.com, a media publisher with an emphasis on men's content. I also assist with growing their Facebook page that has 1.3 million likes.

I formerly made product & tutorial videos for BikeBerry & GrowAce. I actually got the job because the owner surprisingly liked my YouTube videos (www.youtube.com/EngineeredTruth).

Below are samples of my work

Moped GP - Highlights (Music Video)

Is a Prestigious University Really Worth It?

Day in the Life: Los Angel...

Fox E-Scooter - Most Affor...

Motorized Bike Compilati...

The profile picture is big. Employers always want a certain look even if it's borderline unethical. They want someone that looks like they maintain themselves, preferably clean cut.

LinkedIn allows for people to include links to their work (similar to what I already encourage people to do on their regular resume). LinkedIn is cool because it allows people to control their sections. It lets people of all careers cater it to their industry.

Credibility. In general, people trust LinkedIn accounts more than a resume because LinkedIn accounts are public. Anyone who lies on their profile risks getting caught by their friends or coworkers.

LinkedIn allows people to write blogs, which can help create opportunities when people read them.

Here are some tips to start off strong:

Wear at least business casual in your picture. The background of the picture can either be a flat wall, or it can be something professional such as a school, nature, or an office.

Don't make yourself flustered by trying to make it perfect. My LinkedIn was terrible in the beginning, but over time I kept making it better and better. Now, I think it's pretty good. Go ahead and add me: www.LinkedIN.com/in/MatthewTran.

Don't put your classes anywhere near the top. In my opinion, putting your classes on LinkedIn doesn't help. I'm not sure why LinkedIn pestered me for months to put all my classes on there. It never had any results.

LINKEDIN
PROFILE

James Samir Shamsi   1st

Start-up Advisor | Growth Hacker | Owner of
Chameleon.LA | Pokemon Enthusiast

Greater Los Angeles Area | Marketing and Advertising

Current	GNARBOX, Chameleon (www.Chameleon.LA), Jumpcut Studios
Previous	The Economist, Marketing, Advertising & Branding Association London, Beattie McGuinness Bungay
Education	King's College London, U. of London

Send a message ▼

500+
connections

Posts

Published by James Samir

1,096
followers

Secretly, I'm A HOT GIRL On LinkedIn - Here's...
July 8, 2015

How I Made $2,000+ with a 10-second Snapchat
January 29, 2015

Getting Yourself/Your Brand On The News
January 19, 2015

Background

 Summary

"Genius" - Ryan Holiday
"A great person" - My mom.
"Shamsi is a social media maven"- Elite Daily
"Shamsi is doing Gods work" - The Daily Beast
"A young specialist in social networks" - The Huffington Post

---

▶ Learn how to go viral & growth hack your brand: www.JamesSamirShamsi.com

---

Hi,

I'm James, Im 22 and moved to LA to see what the sun looks like -- I also make stuff go viral.
Send me a joke: jamesshamsi@gmail.com

Take pictures of all of your achievements and accomplishments. People love pictures (which is why Instagram is so popular). Make it easier for people to absorb who you are and what you've done by posting pictures of it.

If you want a great example of a LinkedIn profile, check out the profile of my close friend James: https://www.linkedin.com/in/jamessamirshamsi.

People find him and offer him jobs and gigs all the time via LinkedIn. Now that we have all the necessary material prepared, let's move on to the next big step: Applying for jobs.

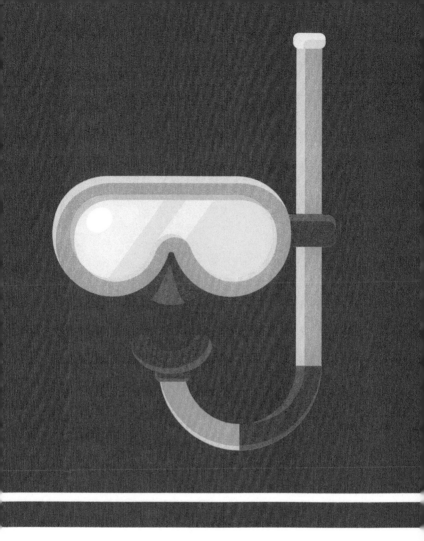

**CHAPTER 4 //
Where To Look**

Where To Look //
Experience that Actually Helps

The 3-2-1 Method of Working at Your Dream Company

Most people have an ideal company they'd like to work for. Facebook, Google, or Buzzfeed are common names thrown out there. Unfortunately, a lot of grown adults also want to work for these companies; your chance of going straight into your dream company is slim - unless you did exceptionally well in college.

For most people (including me), you'll have to go through the 3-2-1 method of getting to your dream company/job. The 3-2-1 method is simple. You're going to work at a Tier 3 company (small company), then at a Tier 2 company (medium sized company), and then at a Tier 1 (ideal/large company). Not everyone's goal is to work for a large company, but the concept is the same regardless. The basic idea is that we're going to start off working at a less desirable company and gradually move to a desirable company. Go to your dream company's career website and look at the positions they hire for. Find your ideal job and apply for that job.

JOB
OPENINGS

ADMIN

Facilities Coordinator

Office Coordinator

Receptionist

BUSINESS OPERATIONS

Account Coordinator

Account Manager

Account Planner

Account Strategist

Likely, you won't get it unless you have significant experience; grown adults with 3+ years of experience are applying for the same position. But all isn't lost. You're going to work your way up to getting three to five years of experience so that you can have a competitive shot.

Find the exact same position at a small company that does something similar. For example, if you want to work at Google, find a smaller software company that has a product similar to one of Google's products. If you want to work for Buzzfeed, find a smaller publisher that also posts articles. Typically, you want to aim for companies with 50 or less employees, because these companies will be easier to get a job at. It's significantly more important to get the position that you want than to work for the company that you want. It's pretty easy to change the company you work for. You just apply and hope to get a job. Changing your skillsets and specialization is very hard.

When you get a job at a Tier 3 company, you most likely won't be satisfied with it. Tier 3 companies typically underpay, and increase pay very slowly. Corporate cultures tend to be a hit or miss. Either everyone loves working there, or everyone hates it. A Tier 3 company is not the goal, it's just a stepping stone. For that reason, I highly recommend not being picky when it comes to getting your first job. At this point in your career, you can't be that picky - because you're easily replaced. Once you have more experience, you can be more selective about the work you take.

JOB APPLICATIONS NOWADAYS ARE LIKE:

"WE'RE LOOKING FOR SOMEONE AGED 22-26 —— WITH —— 30 YEARS EXPERIENCE"

Getting Experience Without Experience

One of the most common problems that young job seekers face when looking for employment are entry-level positions that ask for years of experience. A lot of college students get caught up in this. In most cases, employers just want years of experience even if you taught yourself. Here are a few ways to get experience without experience:

School of YouTube

 It's becoming more and more common for people to teach themselves skills from YouTube videos; ranging from welding to programming. I taught myself everything I needed to know about shooting and editing videos from YouTube. Because YouTube is such a competitive place, usually these video tutorials will be better than lectures that you receive in a class you paid for.

Freelance Work

 Once you've gained some skills in whatever you want to do, try finding some freelance work in that field. Some careers are a lot more freelance friendly than others. There are a lot of websites where you can look for freelance work. Here's a short list:

 Fiverr.com

 Craigslist.com

WayUp.com

Freelancer.com

These websites are also useful for feedback. It'll give you an idea of how much you can charge for your skills, and also how much you need to improve to be paid more. The work you do on these sites can be put on your resume, so you can actually have paid work experience.

Shadowing and Volunteering

Not all careers can be learned from videos (e.g. dentist, doctor, nurse, lawyer). In this case, you'll usually have to learn by shadowing or volunteering. Finding a professional to shadow can be intimidating, and especially hard if you're not used to cold contacting people. There are websites like www.shadowdoctor.com which help students link up to professionals, but generally it's best to ask someone you have some sort of relationship with. If you want to shadow a dentist, ask the dentist that you've been going to as a patient. Generally, you want to find a professional that you have some rapport with. To build rapport, just ask them questions about where they went to school, how they like their job, etc. before asking to shadow.

Where to Apply for Your Tier 3 Job

When you're looking for a job, it's important to look on websites that cater to your skill level. Your college career website is the best place to find a job or internship for college students; you know job postings on there are specifically looking for college students. Another place that caters to low experience is craigslist. Job postings there tend to pay less but expect less experience.

I highly recommend applying to every position you qualify for even if you're not interested in working there. A lot of college students will struggle with interviewing, and the only way to get better is by practicing. Interviewing for companies you don't really care for is the best practice you can get; if you're indifferent, then you don't care if you get the position or not. Remember, you can always turn down a position if you really don't want to try it out. In general, companies know that there's a high turnover rate for entry-level positions. If you want to just try a job for a few months then leave, that's perfectly fine. You'll end up with a bit more cash, a bit wiser than before, and maybe some skills you can use down the road.

Where to Apply for a Tier 2 Job

After you get one to four years of experience, it's time to start looking up the food chain. You've most likely learned a lot more about the industry you work in and gained a lot of real life work experience. The hardest part of your career is over, and now you can leverage your experience to get a better position. The best part about looking for a Tier 2 job is that you can comfortably do it while still working at your Tier 1 job. These are the websites that I recommend applying through once you have experience:

LinkedIn.com

Indeed.com

Monster.com

Glassdoor.com

Staffing Agencies

LinkedIn, Indeed, Monster, and Glassdoor get so many applicants that people with little to no experience often get ignored.

If a company doesn't want to look for people for positions that need to be filled, they will usually hire a staffing agency to find people for them. The staffing agency makes money by getting a cut of the potential employee's pay. Most staffing positions are contract-to-hire, meaning you'll work as a contractor for a few months. Depending on your performance and how the company is doing financially, they may bring you on full-time. By submitting your resume to a staffing agency, they will help you find work. Generally, working with staffing agencies is more effective once you have experience.

Where to Look for a Tier 1 Dream Job

Great companies usually try to make it a huge pain in the ass to apply to their company. They usually do this to screen out people who don't really want to work there. Usually, you'll have to apply directly on their website, and there will be a tedious amount of questions that you'll have to answer about yourself. Typically, it's worth a shot to apply to a Tier 1 company once you have three or more years of experience.

CHAPTER 5 //
Interviewing 101

Interviewing 101 //
How to Interview Like a Pro

The interview is the most stressful part of the job process. Now you have to try to sell yourself to someone who is also interviewing several other qualified applicants at the same time. It's also common now for companies to do two to three rounds of interviews before selecting a candidate, which means more opportunities to be disappointed. Doing well in an interview is the same as performing well in any other high pressure situation: It's all about preparation.

Preparing for the Interview

Research

This one is cliché, but necessary. Here's a checklist on how to research a company prior to interviewing:

 Read through every page of the company's website. Especially their mission statement.

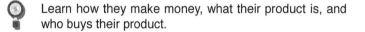 Learn how they make money, what their product is, and who buys their product.

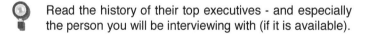 Read the history of their top executives - and especially the person you will be interviewing with (if it is available).

What to Wear

It's important to wear a complete fitted suit to an interview. Acceptable suit colors are: black, navy, and dark grey. The shirt should be a fairly neutral color such as white, light blue, grey, etc. Generally, you don't want to wear a black shirt because that's more for funerals or servers. Women should wear a blazer that follows the same color scheme. Some suites are glossy and reflect, but those are not what you want for an interview. Be sure to choose a matte suite. The only time it's okay to wear business casual to an interview is if it's something minimum wage and/or part-time; such as McDonalds, Starbucks, etc.

Anticipate Questions

After you've interviewed for a few companies, you can somewhat predict what they'll ask. Read through the job requirements, and try to guess what they'll ask you. They'll ask how you're qualified to fulfill each task for the role that you're applying for. They will also ask you general questions about your personality and goals. A lot of companies want to make sure that you'll be happy working at that company. Those companies check to see if you're legitimately interested in their product and if you'd get along with the current employees. Here's a short list of common questions:

 Why do you want to work at this company?

 Can you tell me about what you've worked on before?

 What are your long-term career goals?

 If you were hired, how would you handle this project?

General Tips

Show up at least 10 minutes early– ideally somewhere between 15 to 25 minutes early.

Don't drink caffeine before the interview; you'll usually end up talking too fast.

Shave before the interview. A beard might impress the ladies, but it'll usually come off as unprofessional to an employer. A short beard is typically okay.

Be sure your handshake is firm. When you do shake hands, look the person in the eye.

Stand tall. Practice perfect posture for a few days prior to the interview.

 Don't make any jittery or nervous movement, such as tapping your leg.

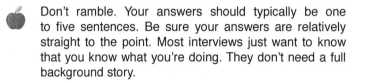 Don't ramble. Your answers should typically be one to five sentences. Be sure your answers are relatively straight to the point. Most interviews just want to know that you know what you're doing. They don't need a full background story.

 Let your humor show a bit. If you're a naturally funny person, it's good to crack a few light jokes. Just don't poke fun at the company you're interviewing for. Making the interviewer laugh builds a huge amount of rapport and demonstrates social intelligence.

 Bring copies of your resume, any supporting data for your achievements and accomplishments (graphs and charts are a good idea), and the best samples of your work.

Interviewing for a Small Company

Interviewing for a small company is different from interviewing for a large company. Small companies usually have very informal interviews that feel more like a conversation. Here are some general tendencies of an interview with a small company:

 They'll go over your resume, so be sure you can elaborate on every point you've made.

You'll likely be meeting with the owner of the company during the hiring process.

It's more based on cultural fit than your capabilities. Each team member has a huge influence on the social environment.

 Be prepared to handle multiple roles.

 Some small companies are in a hurry to hire, so be sure to schedule your interview ASAP, and be prepared to be offered the position on the spot.

Interviewing for a Large Company

Interviewing for large companies can be intimidating. Here are some of their common habits:

 Multiple panel interview. You may have two to three people interviewing you at a time.

 Several rounds of interviews. You might have a phone interview, then do a few on-site interviews.

 Structured questions. A large company might have a set of questions that they ask every applicant, then ask personalized questions after the pre-planned questions.

 More interested in your capabilities, but cultural fit is still a concern.

 It'll likely be a long hiring process that can take a few months.

 Be prepared to have a thorough background check and drug test.

Conclusion

Interviewing is a hard skill to learn. Sometimes you've already lost before you even step in the door, because there's a much more qualified candidate. There are special occurrences where people land the first job that they interview for, but that won't be most people. I was rejected from eight internships before landing one. After every rejection, I would pace in front of my dorm for 30 minutes, figuring out what I could've done better. Reflecting on my previous mistakes helped me interview a bit better each time, and helped me cope with the stress. The best thing you can do is see it as a game, and try not to get too discouraged every time a company hires someone else over you.

CHAPTER 6 //
Money Talks

Money Talks //
Learning how to Negotiate and Leverage
Yourself

If all went well up until this point, you should have a job offer. If things went really well, then you'll have multiple job offers. To be honest, negotiating at this stage of your career will usually not get you anywhere. Most entry-level candidates are easily replaced, so companies usually have a set salary that they give to all their entry-level employees. They also don't want all the entry-level employees to complain about someone getting paid more than them. Even though it's pretty hard to negotiate a better package, there are ways to do it.

Get Multiple Offers

The best way to negotiate is to get multiple offers, then pit those offers against each other. I encourage people to apply and interview for positions they qualify for, but aren't interested in. The point isn't to get a job that you know you'll hate, but to use that offer to negotiate for a better offer at the job you actually want. Employers won't take your negotiation seriously unless you're willing to walk away for a better offer. There are a couple of psychological things going on when you get multiple offers:

- When you have multiple offers, you won't come off as needy. It's easy to be confident when multiple companies want you to work for them. The parallels to this and dating are uncanny.

- When you tell a company that you have other offers on the table, it instantly raises your perceived value. 'Other companies want to hire this person, so there must be something about him/her that is valuable.'

It's important to try to get your offers at about the same time. Usually when a company offers you a job, they want you to accept as fast as possible. They want to stop searching and move along with the hiring process. I recommend asking when they need a response by. No matter what their answer is, you should ask for a week to accept. The typical response I give is something like this: "Wow, I'm very excited about this offer, but I don't like to make major decisions in the moment. Can I get a week to think about this offer?" You generally shouldn't make a company wait more than a week for a response. They may want a response in a few days. If you think that's reasonable, then go for it.

Should You Take a Job Offer on the Spot?

I've taken one job on the spot. I knew it was exactly what I wanted, and I had been unemployed for several months, so I wasn't in a situation to be picky. I ended up not regretting it. It was my first job in media, and I happily worked there for nine months. I ended up walking away with a greater skillset, which opened doors to higher paying positions in media.

However, most people will recommend not to take a job on the spot. Here are a couple of reasons why:

- If a company offers to hire you on the spot, it most likely means the position is not that great. Companies that are great to work for are usually very picky, and will make their hiring process as big of a pain as possible to weed out people.

- You give up a lot of your negotiating power. By asking for a week to think about the offer, you can wait for other offers to trickle in, then pit them against each other. If you take an offer on the spot, you usually won't be able to negotiate as well.

There are situations where it's okay to accept a position on the spot. If you really want that job and think they are offering you a fair deal, then just take it. I don't see the point in playing games for the sake of playing games.

Experience and Accomplishments

The second best negotiating tools are experience and accomplishments. If you have extraordinary accomplishments and experience, you may be rare enough that you can use those to negotiate a better deal. However, this argument is still a lot weaker than having multiple offers. A lot of recruiters are good at shutting down the experience and accomplishment argument with, "Unfortunately, we don't have the budget to offer you more," or, "We start everyone at the same pay. That is our company policy."

Companies are Flexible in Different Areas

Each company has a different set of values, and based on those values, some things are easier to negotiate for than others. Depending on how the interview goes, consider negotiating for the following:

 More vacation days

 Flexible hours

 Ergonomic desk, and chair

 Dual monitors (this is absolutely crucial to be effective)

 Delayed start (Give yourself a week to relax before starting a full-time job. You usually don't want to take a vacation for the first six months of working at a job, so take a vacation before you start working.)

Performance bonuses (Companies are much more willing to give bonuses than a higher salary– especially if the bonuses are based on performance.)

Work remotely on certain days

Each company will be flexible in different areas. If they hint that they have flexible hours, poke at it even more and ask for more flexibility. If they're inflexible in certain areas (e.g. dress code), then don't bother poking at an area where they have hard rules.

General Negotiating Tips

Have a salary in mind when you interview. Tools like glassdoor.com, indeed.com, and payscale.com will give you an idea of what you should be paid. Keep in mind, whatever salary you ask for, you have to earn more than that amount of money for the company to make it worth it for them to hire you. I generally pick exactly how much value I think I can add or a bit more. I usually don't go more than $5,000 over what I think I can earn for the company. It's good to have a minimum amount you're willing to take, along with the ideal realistic amount you want.

The mood of a negotiation is different than the mood of an interview. An interview should be light, energetic, fun, and smooth. A negotiation is calm, slow, methodical and deliberate. I recommend most people to not throw any jokes during negotiations; it's a touchy conversation.

Negotiating shows competence. People who are confident and know their value will argue for the pay they deserve. By trying to negotiate, you're telling the employer that you know your value and that you're not desperate for just any job. It's a huge sign of competence. I've walked away from a few jobs because they offered to pay below what I was looking for. In several cases, the employer came back and asked me how much I was looking for. I've never had someone rescind an offer because I negotiated for better pay.

- Don't talk about salary until they give you an offer. It's fairly common for companies to lowball you (offer you a much lower salary than what they should give you). Don't be shocked, disappointed, or angry when they lowball you, this is just a standard practice and the beginning of the negotiation.

- Control the timing by just communicating. The chances of you getting all your offers in the exact same week is unlikely. If you are in a multiple round interview process with Pepsi, but Coke offers you a job in the middle of the process, then tell Pepsi that you got an offer. The script can go something like this:

  "Hi John, I've appreciated the opportunity to interview so far. I really want to work for Pepsi, but Coke has given me an offer, and I need to get back to them in a week. Is there any way we can expedite this process?"

Conclusion

If you have no work experience, you probably won't be able to negotiate for better pay. That's okay, because at that point of your career, getting experience is more valuable than pay. For your first real job, it's okay to take a bad deal. It's common for people to leave jobs after six months, and generally it is the accepted standard for people to leave after a few years. You can be more firm about your demands later on when you already have a decent job, but are looking for a better one.

CHAPTER 7 //
Life After College

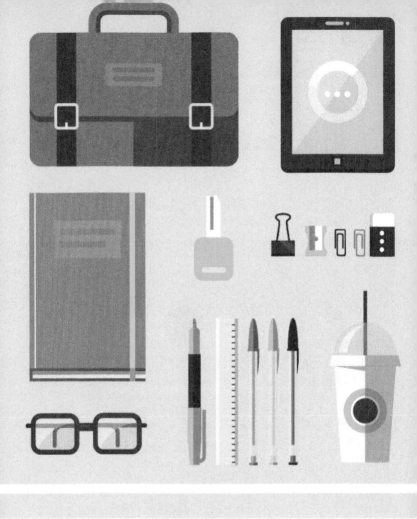

Life After College //
Adjusting to the Real World

Adjusting to life after college can be rough. After I graduated from Mechanical Engineering school, I went from being surrounded by friends all the time, to being surrounded by coworkers. When I worked as an engineer, most of my coworkers were annoying to work with. I usually only had one friend at work, and hated being there. The work I was doing was boring, and the people I worked with were just as boring. Fast forward two years, and now I work at a digital media company called Uproxx where I'm much happier with my career. I mostly work remotely (from my computer at home specifically), which allows me to see my friends more often. I even take trips out of town in the middle of the week to see friends! I don't take time off, I just work from my laptop. I would be lying if I told you it was easy to get to where I am. Here's what I had to do:

- I had to quit my engineering career. Even though I got a good GPA in mechanical engineering, and had three engineering jobs under my belt, I decided to throw it all in the trash to start a career in media.

- For six months, I watched YouTube tutorial videos on how to film and edit videos, and then practiced on my own YouTube channel (I never paid a single penny for an online course). After I got pretty good, I got a job off craigslist to make videos at BikeBerry.com for $15 an hour.

- I worked there for nine months to improve my skills. Now, my income is nearly double what it was.

- Now I'm getting contracts to do social media for a number of different clients, most of them being large YouTube channels. (One client I have right now is Bro Science Life, a channel with more than 1 million subscribers.) Our contracts run from a thousand a month to a few thousand per month. I am pretty good at what I do.

Here's What I Gained in the Past Two Years:

- I'm not afraid of getting fired from any job. I can sustain myself on my YouTube income. The contracts I get are just money on top of that.

- I can work mostly from home, which gives me a flexible schedule. I rarely set an alarm.

- I find my work to be rewarding, because I'm directly entertaining or educating people.

- When I tell people what I do, they tend to be really interested. I'm often the center of attention at dinner. I enjoy being the center of attention.

Here's What I Had to Sacrifice for Two Years:

1. For six months, I barely made enough money to get by, even when living with my parents. I didn't make enough money to go on dates. I was ashamed about the amount I made. I didn't go on dates until I got the job at BikeBerry, but after that it got a lot better.

2. My friends and parents thought I was crazy. They didn't think very highly of me during this time. They thought I was chasing a dream that was never going to happen. I could oddly relate to rappers and musicians that were still in the grind. This wasn't easy, but it gave me motivation to make it.

In retrospect, it was the best leap of faith I have ever taken, and I'm absolutely happy that I did it. For anyone that hates their job: Save up money, figure out what you're going to do next, and take the leap.

Master's degree: Useful or not?

If you're struggling with finding your career, it's tempting to rush straight into a master's degree. I was tempted to when I was about to graduate college. Before deciding if a master's degree will be worth it for you, try these steps first.

1. Go to job posting websites, such as indeed.com or monster.com, and look for positions that require the master's degree you want to pursue. If the degree is very specialized, you may need to check out job posting websites dedicated to that niche. If you can't find a good number of job postings that require your preferred master's degree, it's a good indicator that the master's won't help you much in your job search.

2. Email or meet with people that work in the industry and ask them if a master's degree would be helpful. You can see if there's a group for that industry on Meetup.com, or you can join an association (e.g.: Society of Petroleum Engineers, American Association of Mechanical Engineers).

3. Try getting a job in the industry first before getting a master's degree. Getting a job in the industry will give you a good idea whether a master's will actually be beneficial. Some companies will give you a higher salary if you have a master's, while many will not. Usually, if you can get your foot in the door without a master's, it's best not to get one. The time and effort can be used to accelerate your career by working instead of going back to school.

It's important to not rush straight into a master's program, as it's becoming more and more common that people with a master's degree work at jobs they could have gotten without it. It's fairly embarrassing to be the person with a master's at an entry-level job. Here are some reasons you should get a master's:

1. You got accepted into an elite master's program for a practical master's (e.g.: engineering, MBA, physician's assistant, nursing).

2. There's high demand for the career that you want, but you need a master's for it (e.g.: physicists).

3. The company you work for rewards people with master's degrees and helps pay for the program with tuition reimbursement.

4. You want to switch careers.

Here are reasons you should not get a master's degree:

1. You got a liberal arts degree (e.g.: English, sociology, philosophy) and you believe that the only way you can get a job in those fields is by getting a master's. In most cases, you will still not be able to get a job in those industries even with a master's. Be especially careful if you plan to go to Law school. The growing number of Law graduates that complain about getting a job is alarming.

2. You can't get a job in your industry so you think a master's will help you land a job. If you can't get a job after college, it most likely has more to do with your strategy and credentials than the degree that you have. I strongly suggest revamping your resume, cover letter, credentials, and interview skills instead of getting a master's. Even if you got a less useful degree, you can still apply for general jobs that don't require a specific degree. These jobs can lead to great careers.

Unfortunately, master's degrees are becoming less and less relevant because many colleges update their curriculum slower than they should. Elon Musk, the founder of Paypal, Tesla, SpaceX, and SolarCity, dropped out of his master's of physics program.

Friends

Having a social life after college can be hard. In college, I hung out with people every day. Everybody had time and it was convenient. After college, people get busy with work and spread out from each other, making it much harder to meet up. Most of your acquaintances will fall to the wayside, and you'll only hang out with about five of your friends after college. Despite attending college for more years than most people, I only talk to about 10 college friends. Though it's the harsh reality of life after college, it's possible for your social life to be better after college. Here are some things that I did:

- When I really wanted to make friends, I joined a bunch of groups on Meetup.com. It's a website where people can join different groups, each holding their own events. People that join these groups are open to making new friends, which make them a great place to make friends. I tried out a few, and eventually found one that fit me the best. There were a couple of months where I was going to a meetup every day; I hated my job so much that I wanted an escape. This will take more effort and social skills than meeting people in college, but it is worth it. Well, usually worth it. There are some awkward groups on Meetup.com.

- My friends and I don't hang out as much as we used to, but when we do, we can actually afford to do fun stuff. My group usually goes on a few trips a year, typically on a cruise or a trip to Las Vegas.

- I highly recommend joining a niche gym (e.g. crossfit, MMA, rock-climbing) over a typical gym (e.g. 24 Hour Fitness, LA fitness). Not only are they more fun, but people tend to make friends at niche gyms, whereas nobody talks to each other at typical gyms. In my opinion, they're absolutely worth the extra costs.

Making a Good Impression (Your First 90 Days)

Making a good first impression at a job sets the foundation for your role and respect in the company. Here are some ideal things you want to do in your first 90 days:

 Surpass any expectations that they set for you.

Sometimes this is impossible because you're in training, and there really isn't a way to exceed expectations - especially in positions where you just maintain the business. Positions where you're in charge of growing the business give you a lot more potential to exceed expectations.

 Solve problems that aren't even assigned to you.

Most companies have some sort of tedious task they need to get done to maintain the business. Most tedious computer tasks can be automated with a simple computer program. I highly recommend learning coding on the side (I know how to casually code in a few languages and it has helped me a ton). If you're not the coding type, you can easily pay for a freelancer to make a code for you. You'd be surprised at how cheap basic computer programs are (e.g. Craigslist.com, Freelancer.com, Fiverr.com).

Don't question the way things are done.

It's okay to automate a way something is done, but it's not okay to give suggestions that completely change the way things are done. In college, professors typically encourage students to debate and discuss topics. Many of you will find that your boss won't be so encouraging. Most companies have a set way of doing things, and have been doing it that way for several years. Even though it's an inefficient way to do things now, it probably made sense at one point. After you earn their respect, you can start giving more influential suggestions.

Keep in mind, this just applies for most companies. There are companies out there who encourage all their employees to throw in suggestions no matter how long they've been with the company.

 Go to every social event that you're invited to.

Every time I start a new job, I try to go to every social event I'm invited to. When I enjoy being around my coworkers, work goes from "I hate being here" to "I'm hanging out with friends." The best way to build friendships is by hanging out outside of work - preferably with drinks, lots of drinks. **But my coworkers are so old! They're all married and have kids :(**

If you thought age gaps were drastic in college... SURPRISE! You most likely have coworkers who have children that are your age. The odds of you being the youngest person at a company are surprisingly high. I was usually the youngest at most of the companies I started working for. It's definitely harder to connect with older employees. You may never become best friends with them, but you can still crack jokes and have a good time. Socializing with people in their 30s, 40s, and 50s takes some adjusting. Here are some tips when it comes to talking to your more seasoned coworkers:

Avoid talking about their children, unless they bring it up. You can't really relate to it, and it just makes the age gap feel ridiculous.

Asking them for advice is a good way to show respect and it also breaks the ice. Start with asking them for advice about work, then once a friendship is built, start asking for advice about life (e.g. investing, saving for retirement, marriage, buying a house). People love giving advice.

Don't talk about your personal life too much. Unfortunately, most of your older coworkers won't be able to relate to your desire to go to Coachella, the biggest music festival west of the Mississippi.

Socializing with coworkers can prevent you from being let go.

When companies choose who to let go, the two prime factors in their decision are performance and likeability. Employers weigh these two aspects differently; some put an emphasis on performance, while others rank likeability as a priority. Either way, these are the top two factors in keeping a job - so it's best to start making conversation when you can.

Moving on After Your First Job

If you're like the majority of millennials, your first job sucks. You're likely underpaid, and your responsibilities involve looking at an excel sheet until your eyeballs dry out. If you're unhappy with your job after the first three months, it's time to start looking for employment elsewhere. But wait, isn't three months too soon to leave? Won't that make me look bad? Your parents would probably tell you that, but times are a bit different now. It's super common for people to leave companies at any time now. Let's be real, most employers have no problem letting you go after three months if they don't like you, so you shouldn't feel bad about leaving either. Searching for a new job can take months, so start as early as possible. Luckily, with your three months of experience, you're slightly more valuable than before (Sweet!). Test the job market to see what you can get - you might surprise yourself.

Leaving a Job Appropriately

It's important to leave all employers on a good note. When I left BikeBerry, I gave my employer a one month notification, and offered to help hire and train my replacement. After I left, the owner of the company told me I was welcome back at any time. Since then, I've never had to worry about being unemployed; I'll always have a job available to me. I really appreciate the offer my former boss gave me. His offer still gives me a feeling of security. Here's how you keep the doors open:

 Give at least two weeks notice before you leave. If necessary, stay an additional few weeks to finish any projects.

 Offer to help hire and train your replacement. If you're a specialist, you most likely know things about your role that your boss doesn't know. You're the best person to hire and train your replacement. Make your departure from the company as seamless as possible.

"But if you train your replacement, doesn't that mean you can't go back?"

Companies never want to stay the same size, all companies want to grow. If a company has one engineer, they want two engineers as soon as possible. If an employer likes you, they will make room for you somewhere. Good employees are hard to come by.

 Treat your former employer to dinner. Leaving a company can be sad and scary for both sides. Have a dinner with your former employer to have one last casual conversation before you go. Both of you probably have things that you want to say before you depart. I also try to have dinner with any of the coworkers I got along with.

CONCLUSION

After I got fired from all 3 of my engineering jobs, I was in a depressing dip in my life. Fast forward 2 years later, I have a career that allows me to work from home, and I get excited when I get to work on new projects. I even have the luxury of turning down projects that don't interest me.

The first few years of your adult work life will be rough. It can be especially daunting when some of your friends start off with shockingly high salaries while you remain unemployed (I've been there). It's perfectly normal for someone to take 2-3 years to figure out what they want to do with their life. It's a big decision that should have a lot of thought behind it.

If you're quitting a traditional career for a career that was only created in the past few years, then you're most likely making a good decision. Most of your friends and family will think that you're making a poor decision because they're a bit behind in their career knowledge, but once they see that you have financial stability, they'll change their minds (my friends and family certainly did).

When you're searching for a fulfilling career, you shouldn't have to force yourself to like a job. Employers love to see applicants that have relevant side projects because it's a genuine sign of experience and passion. And the only way someone can complete impressive side projects is by being naturally interested in the subject.

Employers worry that applicants are lying on their resume. Try out of the box ways to prove that you know what you're doing. Show them your YouTube channel, Instagram account, or articles that you've written. A bit of unconventional proof goes a long way.

My hope is that you don't envision 'finding your dream job' to be a daunting rite of passage into adulthood. I want you to see it as a game. When you're first figuring out the rules, it's not going to be fun, but after you get good enough to where you're beating other people, then it's a blast.

If you want further career information, feel free to check out my YouTube channel: YouTube.com/EngineeredTruth.

THE JOB SEEKERS CHECKLIST

☐ Purchase professional attire.

☐ Clean up any embarrassing social media.

☐ Create a professional email.

☐ Get your hair cut and/or your beard trimmed.

☐ Update your resume (focus on the most career-relevant info).

☐ Upload resume to your Indeed/ Monster account.

☐ Create a LinkedIn account.

☐ Go to a job fair, network!

- [ ] Compile a list of job opportunities.

- [ ] Write job-specific cover letters.

- [ ] Send out applications.

- [ ] When you get an interview, learn about the company.

- [ ] Practice saying "yes" instead of "yeah".

- [ ] Get a few references lined up.

- [ ] Print several copies of your resume for the interview.

- [ ] Turn off your cell phone before going in.

- [ ] Be yourself!

- [ ] Send a polite email follow-up with the interviewer.

- [ ] If you don't get an offer, ask for feedback.

- [ ] Hang in there!

GETTING TO KNOW YOUR SKILLS

Getting to know what you want out of your life is one of the most important journeys you will ever go on. This final section of the book is more of a workbook. Here you can interact with everything you've read and then put it to the test.

First off, begin by assessing yourself. In this skills challenge below, we'll cover the BIG 4: People, Technical, Leadership and Problem Solving. Make sure to be completely honest with yourself; even if that means leaving some sections blank. Keep in mind all the tasks that you have employed during your past. Not just in previous jobs, but when you've volunteered, at home and in school.

People Skills

List 5 Examples of You Using People Skills in the Last Year:

1

2

3

4

5

Technical Skills

List 5 Examples of You Using Technical Skills in the Last Year:

1

2

3

4

5

Leadership Skills

List 5 Examples of You Using Leadership Skills in the Last Year:

1

2

3

4

5

Problem Solving Skills

List 5 Examples of You Using Problem Solving Skills in
the Last Year:

1

2

3

4

5

GETTING TO KNOW YOURSELF

Again, the most important thing here is to be honest with yourself. What is your current lifestyle like? Do you wake up in the afternoon, are you binge-watching Netflix all day? What are your hobbies?

When you have a few minutes, a couple hours or an entire day for yourself, what do you enjoy doing the most?

What are chores, activities or classes that you took in the past that you simply hated?

GETTING TO KNOW YOUR DREAMS

What's your dream job? Regardless of degree, money, hours, travel, what's the one thing you could see yourself doing for the rest of your life?

Do you have a dream house, dream car, dream family? Is there anywhere in the world where you would love to live, regardless of what career you're doing?

Is there a nightmare job for you? What careers would you hate to have to do for the next 40 + years of your life?

ASSESS YOURSELF:
YOUR NOTES

Use the next few pages as a log. Detail jobs you apply for, interviews you go to, ideas you have. Pretty much anything related to working, hobbies and happiness. Once all the notes are filled out, go back and read through them. These honest reflections will allow you to understand who you are what it is that you want to get out of your career.

118

AUTHOR BIO

Matt Tran has worked in the Natural Gas, Oil, and HVAC Industry. He now works as a Social Media Manager for UPROXX, a media publisher that is ranked in the top 100 U.S. websites. He saw that career knowledge on the internet was inadequate and that most college career advisers are underwhelming. He created his YouTube channel Engineered Truth in 2011 with the goal of giving realistic career information. Engineered Truth is now the largest career channel on YouTube with 60,000 subscribers and growing.

CPSIA information can be obtained at www.ICGtesting.com
Printed in the USA
BVOW11s1942250116

433886BV00001B/1/P